.... it's just

PRAIRIE

Ron Richardson 547/1500

..... it's just PRAIRIE

Photography and text by Ron Richardson

Here and There Publishing
Wynyard, Saskatchewan

Here and There Publishing
P.O. Box 1597
Wynyard, Saskatchewan
Canada
S0A 4T0

All photographs, including cover, by Ron Richardson
Book design by Ron Richardson and Heike Gauer
Cover design by Ron Richardson and Steve Penner

First Edition

Printed and bound in Canada by
Friesens
Altona, Manitoba
R0G 0B0

Canadian Cataloguing in Publication Data

Richardson, Ron, 1943 -
     -- It's just prairie

1st ed.
ISBN 0-9680420-0-7

     **1. Richardson, Ron, 1943- 2. Prairie Provinces--
Pictorial works. 3. Landscape photography--Prairie
Provinces. 4. Nature photography--Prairie Provinces.
I. Title**

FC3234.2.R52 1996   779'.36712'092 C96-900183-5
F1060.5.R52 1996

Quotations from recorded albums by Connie Kaldor
reprinted by permission of Connie Kaldor and Coyote Productions.
Thanks.

Previous page: *Sandhill Cranes at
dusk, winging their way back to the
safety of the Quill Lakes for the night.
During migration in the spring and
fall, thousands of cranes, geese,
and ducks spend days or even weeks
fattening up on spilled or unharvested
grain, or at feeding stations and lure
crops set up by the North American
Waterfowl Management Plan.*

▶   *Sometimes a roll of film and
a bit of wild experimenting pays off.
Here I've used a blue gel and a time
exposure of rapids in a northern river
to produce a* **watercolor** *effect.*

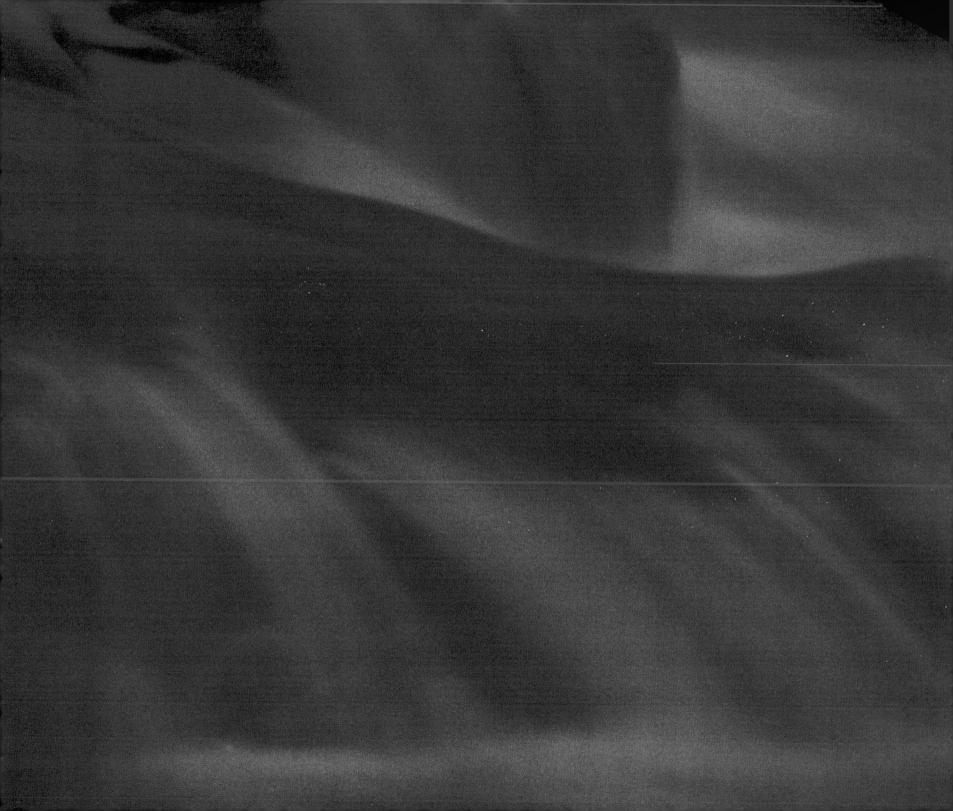

Last of the garden variety Sweet Peas, caught in full bloom by an early snowfall. The heavy, wet snow covered most of the garden greenery as well as many still unharvested crops. Even after drying out, these crops are much harder to pick up and combine.

To Libby

for her unconditional support

for her many hours of help matting and framing

for her help with countless shows and sales

but most of all

for her keen eye

and constructive criticism.

Her unbiased judgment helps make every exposure I print

into the very best photograph it can be.

Acknowledgments

The contributions of many people have gone into the preparation and production of this book.

First of all I thank wildlife photographer Pat Gerlach for showing me, in the beginning, what can be done with transparencies when they are printed properly, then helping me set up my darkroom to do it.

A special thank-you to Hans Dommasch at the University of Saskatchewan. His timely advice and encouragement helped build self-confidence that led to a much greater awareness of my abilities.

Thank you also to my family for their support and help, especially to Libby and to my children, Travis, Kyla, and Taya, who helped out in various ways, both in getting ready for shows and in getting the book ready for printing.

A big thank-you to Marilyn for her advice and help with the lyric quotations, and to Heike for her knowledge and the use of her computer in typesetting the book.

Thank you to Friesens for their very professional and competent help throughout the whole printing process.

Finally, a big thank-you to all the friends, relatives, and acquaintances who offered their support, advice and encouragement, and who helped in the final selection of photos to be included in this book.

A stalk of wheat. Typical of the prairies, right? If this stalk looks a little too perfect it's because it is the world's largest wheat sculpture, in the town of Sceptre, gateway to the Great Sand Hills of southwestern Saskatchewan. Note the sparrows and nest on the right "head of grain".

Introduction

Over and over we hear the phrase, "Who would want to live on the prairie? It's nothing but flat, boring farmland." Even we who live here often fail to see the beauty that is all around us.

In this book I have tried to record some of that beauty for both present and future enjoyment.

Some of the scenes I have recorded are common occurrences that we see every day; others are fleeting glimpses of nature that most of us might see only once in a lifetime. Other scenes are fast disappearing from our landscape because of changing lifestyles and different priorities than our parents and grandparents had.

We can find beauty and interest in almost anything if we just take the time to look for it. We need to see that beauty in our surroundings so that we can learn to take better care of them. Take that time out of your busy schedule to look around you and find some of your own special memories. Even if you only record them in your mind, they will be yours forever.

In order to find that inspiration, however, you may first need to spend some quiet time with this book. Open it frequently and study it carefully. Hopefully you will feel some of the same emotion and enjoyment that I felt while capturing these images.

The geometry of the flat prairie landscape is evident from the air and sometimes can be almost mesmerizing. In the fall the rich golds and browns of harvest and fallow fields lend an additional beauty in the early morning light.

What Is The Prairie?

Prairie – An extensive area of flat or rolling grassland.

Those of us who live on the prairies tend to expand that definition to include areas of bush and poplar. For this book I have also included lakes and forest, sparsely covered badlands, shifting sand dunes, and unique areas like the Cypress Hills of southern Saskatchewan and Alberta. To me these areas cannot be isolated from the prairie geography – they are all part of the same landscape.

Photographs for this book have been collected from as far east as the Ontario border and as far west as the foothills of the Rockies; from the parklands on the edge of the Boreal forests in the north to the badlands of South Dakota in the south – a vast area of great diversification in landform, flora and fauna, weather, and moods, but all part of what is generally known as **the prairies.**

Sometimes I was lucky enough to catch a fleeting image by just being in the right place at the right time. Often I had to spend hours, or even days, waiting for that moment to happen.

Sometimes even a wide angle lens could not capture the whole image seen with the naked eye, as with sunsets which seem to literally surround us. At other times it would take an extreme closeup lens to capture the minute detail of a tiny spring flower.

Quite often the best time to get a good photograph seemed to be at the most inopportune moment, or when the weather was at its absolute worst – a vicious thunder or hail storm on a hot, muggy summer afternoon; a cold winter morning with delicate, beautiful hoarfrost; or a heavy midwinter snowstorm. It's at times like these that a photographer must have that little extra bit of dedication to get those special images. When the quality of light is exceptional, it gives a magical sense and feeling to an otherwise ordinary scene. Light can be everything.

Frequently I did not get the picture I was looking for, but seldom did I consider my time wasted. The beauty was there even if I wasn't able to capture it on film.

A country road on the prairie is sometimes nothing more than a track with no ditches and a barbwire fence overgrown with weeds and prairie grasses.

But oh, oh the road gets longer
The further down it you roam
But oh, oh the feeling gets stronger
For home, home, home

Connie Kaldor from "SLEEPY LITTLE TOWN"

I come from a land that is harsh and unforgiving
Winter snows can kill you
And the summer burn you dry
When a change in the weather
Makes a difference to your living
You keep one eye on the banker
And another on the sky

But oh I get caught by those wide open spaces
Caught by the sight of those straight horizon lines
Caught by the sight of those lined open faces
Weathered over trouble and time
'Cause that big old flatland
She doesn't suffer fools lightly
Watch your step if you're new around
Brown broke down in a blizzard last winter
Tried to walk and froze to death fifty feet from town

But oh I get caught by those blue spring ditches
Farmers seeding hoping it will pay
Hoping that July won't see their hearts
Caught in that topsoil
Watching the wind blow it away

Connie Kaldor from "HARSH AND UNFORGIVING"

Two old barns sit empty as a late winter storm dumps several inches of heavy, wet snow on the rural landscape. It's sad to see so many of these noble structures of the past falling into disrepair; then gradually slipping to their knees before collapsing completely.

A typical prairie landscape but one that may not be around much longer. The big sky will always be here and the stubble and loose straw after the harvest, but the old prairie sentinel is disappearing at an alarming rate.

.... it's just

PRAIRIE

Sunset through the pine trees at Madge Lake campground in Duck Mountain Provincial Park, along the Manitoba/Saskatchewan border. Like most playgrounds on the prairies, it is wonderfully peaceful in the early spring and late fall. Crowds of summer vacationers in July and August fill most parks to overflowing and take away much of that feeling of serenity.

Early morning mist rises from a small beaver pond along the Boiler Creek in Cypress Hills Provincial Park. Scenes like this are the reward for those willing to rise before the sun and brave the chill air to hike the backcountry trails, while others savor the warmth of their cosy sleeping bags.

The prairie is Big Sky Country and the sky is always changing, either because of the time of day or because of weather conditions and constantly changing cloud patterns. The horse appears to have free run of all he surveys as the closed gate behind him seems to stand disembodied from the fence through which it was meant to provide access.

Castle Butte, in the Big Muddy Badlands of south central Saskatchewan, rises sixty meters (200 ft.) above the floor of the Big Muddy Valley. Legend has it that nearby caves were used in the late 1800s as hideouts by rustlers and train robbers such as Butch Cassidy's gang and the Jones-Nelson gang. These outlaws would raid and steal in northern Montana, a lawless part of the country at that time, then retreat across the international border to their hideouts in the badlands.

Spring in the Prairies comes like a surprise
One minute there's snow on the ground
The next there's sun in your eyes
              Connie Kaldor from "SPRING IN THE PRAIRIES"

The Prairie Crocus, or Pasqueflower, is the floral emblem of both Manitoba and South Dakota. It is sometimes quite hard to find these days, as the virgin prairie where it used to grow by the billions has all but disappeared. It can sometimes still be found in abundance on undisturbed hillsides and along unused road allowances. The flower in the photo on the left appears to be a mutated version of the plant. I found it, the only one of its kind, growing on the same hillside as dozens of other ordinary crocuses.

I look to the hills
From whence cometh salvation
I find strength in their quiet roll
And when I feel myself troubled
I look to those hills
And the quiet green quiets my soul
Connie Kaldor from
"HYMN FROM PINCHER CREEK"

▲   *Cypress Hills, Saskatchewan. Fort Walsh was originally built as a North West Mounted Police post in 1875 but was used for only eight years before being abandoned. What was left was destroyed by the great fire of 1886, which also burned all the forest cover from the hills. Reconstruction began in 1942 as a horse breeding and training centre for the R.C.M.P.'s Musical Ride. In 1968 work began to restore the fort to its present condition, representing the 1882 period of its youth.*

▶   *The landscape viewed from Bald Butte Lookout seems to have been painted with a burgundy colored brush. The deep blood red of the setting sun peeking from behind dark clouds to the left of the scene softens the early spring colors, but adds texture due to the low angle of the light source.*

On the South Saskatchewan River
There's a crossing and a bend that they call Batoche
And on the banks of that river
A battle was won and a people were lost
. . .

On the South Saskatchewan River
The crossing and the bend and the banks remain
The people have long since been scattered
Town is still there but it's not the same
But you can hear Gabriel and Riel even yet
They are whispering "You can win what once was lost"
You can hear it in the rustle
Of the poplar leaves
At the bend in the river
They call Batoche
                    Connie Kaldor from "MARIA'S PLACE / BATOCHE"

My family and I visited Batoche several years ago on the hottest Saskatchewan day in recorded history and literally roasted as we explored the battlegrounds, the old townsite, and the cemetery. The only relief from the sun and heat was while we were inside the new museum and interpretive centre. The cemetery contains the graves of Gabriel Dumont, the Métis who were killed in the battle, and many of the original settlers of the Batoche area.

The common Harebell is found on prairie, on cliffs, and on rocky banks throughout most of North America. I photographed this one clinging to the conglomerate cliffs along the edge of the Cypress Hills plateau. Each individual blossom is less than two centimeters (½") across and extremely delicate and perfect.

This Mountain Shooting Star is just one of many unique or rare flowers found in the Cypress Hills. Many of the species are found nowhere else on the prairies; some only on the foothills and slopes of the Rocky Mountains; and some only in the Boreal forests of the North.

A small patch of Black-eyed Susans blooms in a hay field on a warm summer day. Found throughout North America from the Arctic all the way into Mexico, the plant grows abundantly almost anywhere and blooms all summer long.

The Prairie Three-flowered Aven, also known as Prairie Smoke, is still found in abundance on unplowed grassland. In my opinion it is much more beautiful after it has gone to seed. Flowers on the prairies are best photographed very early in the morning, before the summer breezes begin to sway their delicate stems.

Bare poplars on a very still and dark late-winter night. The only light source was a 60 watt back porch bulb, so I had to use a three minute time exposure to make the light-colored tree trunks stand out against the black night behind.

The devastation of a forest fire is not all ugly. The stark contrasting black and white of the burned tree trunks and the colorful regrowth on the forest floor have their own beauty.

Some of the rarest plants found on the prairies are the eighteen species of orchids found in the Cypress Hills. This, the Fairy Slipper or Calypso Orchid, can be found in early spring in open, boggy, wooded areas. Orchids of North America are generally very tiny and grow on the ground rather than on trees as the tropical variety do.

The unopened blossoms (left) are only one and a half centimeters (½ in.) long, and my partner, Libby, found them in the middle of the forest path we were following. Searching the nearby area more closely, we found several more blossoms in gorgeous full bloom.

A cluster of Oyster Mushrooms clings to the bark of an old Boxelder in the garden shelterbelt of my father's farm south of Saskatoon. The afternoon sun, peeking through the foliage above, shone directly on the mushrooms, highlighting them against the dark tree trunk.

A glowing rainbow after a sudden summer storm appears to end on an island in this small lake in the foothills of Alberta. The late afternoon sun skipping under the dark clouds produces a contrasting scene of vibrant color and soft lighting. I wonder if anyone has searched the island for the pot of gold?

Got no home, none to run to
No warm fire, no back yard
Connie Kaldor from "MODERN LULLABY"

A young Striped Skunk gives warning by stamping its front feet . . . time to retreat. This fellow's scent glands were probably not even fully developed yet, but I wasn't about to call his bluff.

A large porcupine, caught in the open and on the ground in broad daylight, scurries to find a tree to climb. Whenever we tried to stop him by putting a branch in front of him, he would turn and give the branch a firm slap with his prickly tail. Upon finding an appropriate tree, he climbed almost to the very top before looking back to watch us leave.

It's 5:00 a.m. on a cool but beautiful late spring morning on the prairies. In a boggy ditch beside a country dirt road grow a large number of gorgeous Yellow Lady Slippers. The bright yellow pouches and reddish-brown spiral side petals provide striking contrast with the dark green leaves and deep shadows cast by the low early-morning sun. The small ridge along the bottom of the single flower (left) makes it look somewhat like a harem slipper.

At one time King of the Prairie, then on the verge of extinction, bison numbers are rebounding as many farmers and ranchers now raise them instead of cattle. Bison are in many ways much easier to take care of than cattle because they are more able to fend for themselves under most harsh prairie conditions. There are still several wild herds in existence, mostly in large parks where they can roam more or less freely over a large uninhabited area. I photographed this big bull in Theodore Roosevelt National Park in North Dakota as he was taking a roll in the buffalo wallow he's still lying in.

While exploring the badlands of South Dakota during late winter, I was driving along the rim road when I spied this small herd of Pronghorn Antelope grazing nearby. As I slowed to observe them and take photos, the animals spooked and began running parallel to the road. I sped up to stay with them and grabbed a lucky shot as they veered away. Antelope are common to most grassland areas of the prairies.

The Prairie Rose or Pasture Rose, Alberta's floral emblem, is a most showy wildflower, especially just after the bloom opens. The intense rose or pink of the new blossom seems to fade quickly, however, and the flowers are difficult to photograph because of their small size and the great abundance of foliage.

26

The Plains Prickly Pear can be found anywhere on the prairies that is dry or sandy. It has tufts of spines each as long as eight centimeters (3 in.) that can be very painful to step on in soft-soled shoes. The short flowering season in late spring produces gorgeous, lush yellow blossoms five to eight centimeters (2-3 in.) in diameter.

*This **icy** scene could have been taken in the Arctic, but in reality it was taken at Little Quill Lake in east central Saskatchewan. The strong prairie winds have pushed the spring ice into piles along the shore.*

The moving ice drags glacial boulders along the bottom of the shallow lake and deposits them at the water's edge. Over thousands of years, with a receding shoreline, the flat plain around the lake has become dotted with boulders varying in size from a few centimeters to more than a meter (a few inches to several feet) in diameter.

The gorgeous Wood Lily, commonly known as the Wild Tiger Lily, grows on undisturbed prairie and in open woods. Because it grows from a bulb and the bulbs are destroyed by plowing, the lily has disappeared from many areas. As a result, large patches like this one (left) are becoming harder to find, even in Saskatchewan, where it is the provincial floral emblem.

A northern sunset. A lake, trees, and peace and quiet. Sometimes we can do no better than to add nothing.

Take me where the loons are calling
Mist in the morning, smell of pine
Whiskey jack wake me up,
Send me out with a fishing line
          Connie Kaldor from "CANOE SONG"

A cool, calm, misty morning at a
northern lake. What a quiet, peaceful feeling
as body and mind become one with nature.

Give me a canoe and let me go
Up past Waskesiu to the Wabinow
Give me a canoe and let me go

Take me where the loons are calling
Lake like glass and a starlit sky
Smell of a small campfire burning,
Sit and watch the embers die
        Connie Kaldor from "CANOE SONG"

Several canoes pulled up on the shore of
Loch Leven, Cypress Hills, add splashes of color
to the quiet early-morning solitude before the
activities of a busy day begin.

A pair of Mallards float quietly on a reedy pond at sunrise. Morning fog adds a misty feeling, which I have enhanced by using a nylon stocking stretched over the paper during printing.

▲   *I spent over an hour flat on my belly, on a very cold fall morning, as this large bull elk paced up and down the hill, trying to get a better view of me and challenging me every minute or so. I wasn't at all sure how serious he was and didn't dare move until he turned his back on me for a few minutes. My fingers were frozen and I had a roll of very dull, contrasty photos because of the poor light conditions. When I arrived back home, I combined one of the photos with a streaky sunset I had taken a few weeks earlier to create a much more striking picture.*

▶   *A mule deer perks her big ears to attention while grazing on tender grasses and small shrubs in the early morning mist. The fog and the pre-dawn light produce a soft, gentle photograph that is easy to feel comfortable with.*

Close your eyes and dream
There are clouds to cuddle
And moonbeams to climb
Connie Kaldor from
"DREAM BABY /
L'ENFANT DES REVES"

▲   *Puffy white clouds add interest to a warm summer sky. Clouds like this sometimes bring much-needed showers but often produce nothing more than a patch of welcome shade.*

▶   *Dark threatening clouds close in over a summer canola field as the sun begins to retreat from the bright yellow flowers. This scene is becoming more typical of the prairies as King Wheat is being increasingly replaced by this newer oilseed crop.*

▲   The simple beauty of a flax field in full bloom.
I waited several hours for the sun to peek out and
highlight the canola and part of the flax while the rest
of the field is still in the shadow of passing clouds.

▶   A typical prairie landscape in early summer
features young crops and fresh summerfallow in the
fields. A very black sky heralds a passing summer
storm.

They sing lullaby, lullaby, coolies and sloughs,
Lullaby, lullaby, coolies and sloughs.
The wind and the willows will whisper to you,
Lullaby, lullaby, coolies and sloughs.
　　Connie Kaldor from "PRAIRIE LULLABY"

▲　　*It is late summer and one of those overcast afternoons when the air is still and close. You just know something is going to happen. The slough is like a mirror and if it weren't for the weeds and bulrushes in the foreground, it would be difficult to tell which way was up.*

▶　　*Golden brown grain fields ripple in the prairie winds. The horse-drawn binders and wagons and the steam-powered threshing machines of yesteryear required many men and long hours to put the crop in the bins. The old house in the distance would have been a beehive of activity during the harvest, as the women of the family washed and cleaned and cooked for the huge threshing crews.*

The Musk or Nodding Thistle is one of many thistles accidentally imported from Europe. It grows to a height of over one meter (3-5 ft.) and the flower can be six to eight centimeters (2-3 in.) in diameter. Like most thistles, the bloom is quite beautiful despite the plant's obnoxious nature.

▲   *Early morning and a sleepy coyote seems unwilling to leave the warm spot he has scratched out amongst the dry buffalo dung. It seemed quite evident he had spent a long, hard night hunting and had just bedded down when I came along to bother him.*

▶   *What fun it was watching this young coyote as he hunted in the long grass for mice and other small animals. He looked almost as if he were playing as he stalked something that only he could see, then pounced with a great leap several feet into the air. I never did see him catch anything.*

The Ground Squirrel, commonly known as the gopher, of which there are several species, ranges over a wide area of North America from desert to mountain valley, and from the sub-tropics to the Arctic. Most Ground Squirrels spend the better part of their lives underground. They retreat into hibernation in late summer and are not seen again until spring.

In farming or cattle country, Ground Squirrels and Prairie Dogs are hunted and poisoned energetically because of the burrows they dig and the grain and grass they supposedly eat. In fact, the burrows help to rejuvenate the soil and the rodents eat many weeds that cattle won't touch.

In earlier times Black-tailed Prairie Dog colonies covered many square miles and contained millions of inhabitants. Today, smaller colonies are confined mainly to grassland park areas, where they can live more or less unmolested by people. Prairie Dogs kiss as a means of recognition and divide their "towns" into neighborhoods that only "residents" are allowed into.

The Great Sand Hills of southwestern Saskatchewan cover an area of nearly two thousand square kilometers (750 sq. mi.). Much of the area is covered with sparse grasses and small cedar and sage bushes, with small clumps of poplar here and there. There is also quite an extensive area of active sand dunes, which are continually shifting with the wind. The moving dunes, some as high as thirty meters (100 ft.) or more, continually bury and smother vegetation in their path, resulting in bare, dry roots and trees being exposed on a regular basis.

Sometimes the wind creates tiny sculptures out of the continually shifting sand. Here the beautiful lines of one of those sculptures are accented by the warm evening rays of the setting sun as it dips toward the horizon.

An old, abandoned farmstead, nestled amongst the summer fields. As with so many old farmyards, the trees and windbreaks have all been bulldozed, leaving the buildings vulnerable to the incessant prairie winds.

Well we sure had our bad times and our fun
And we paid all our taxes to the government of old Saskatchewan
I raised up my kids 'till they finally raised away
And they drop in now and then
To visit on their holidays
Connie Kaldor from "GRANDMOTHER'S SONG"

Driving along a flat prairie highway in a gentle spring rain, I was not thinking much about making photographs, when this old farm, across the fields, caught my eye . I turned around and scouted out a position along a nearby country road where I could take this photo from the car using a long telephoto lens.

Typical of modern prairie transportation, at least for goods and commodities, this long diesel freight speeds along a flat, straight stretch of lonely track. Note that there are eight engines – count the fuel tanks. Because it's a modern train, there is no caboose, although you can't tell from the photograph.

More typical of days gone by is this old steam engine with tender, flat car, box car, and caboose. This scene is now a fixed display at the Western Development Museum in North Battleford. As far as I know, you won't find anything like this being used anywhere on the prairies today. In fact, many of our steam engines were shipped to the Soviet Union, where I saw some of them twenty years ago on the Trans-Siberian Railway.

I go over and over the memories again
Like a ship that is caught on some hidden reef
Looking back I see things in a different perspective
With a knowledge now that I wish I had then

But time's not a stone
It is bright paper tissue
It rips, and it tears
There's no having again
            Connie Kaldor from "THIN THREAD"

At Inglis, Manitoba, west of Riding Mountain National Park, stand these five original grain elevators. Very weathered and painted over several times with new names, they stand in tribute to the many pioneers who hauled their grain here originally in horse-drawn wagons. Poor foundation conditions and uneven loading of the storage bins over the years have contributed to the lean in each structure.

▲ *Sunsets and silhouettes are things I don't often photograph because they are technically not difficult to produce. Occasionally, however, one like this, at Southey, in south central Saskatchewan, results in a very special print.*

When the sun on the prairies is going to sleep,
You can see it turn golden and red in the west,
There's the barest of breeze, in the shelterbelt trees,
Singing each baby to rest.
Connie Kaldor from "PRAIRIE LULLABY"

▶ *This bright red barn, typical of thousands of prairie barns of years gone by, is fast becoming one of a dying breed as most farms have no animals anymore, except pets. The sun, peeking under the dark, rolling storm clouds and shining on the freshly painted boards provides a stunning contrast of color.*

I had to leave,
Try to make a new start,
But how far can you go,
When you don't have your heart
Connie Kaldor from "SASKATOON MOON"

A set of old grain wagon wheels on my father's farm near Saskatoon. I was trying a new film at the time and the color on the slide is absolutely dead, so I went back the next summer to repeat the photos. In the meantime, the area had been cleaned up and everything burned. As a result, I've had to use the "dead" slide and print to revive color as best I could.

One of rural Saskatchewan's many once thriving farmyards – now left to the elements as more and more of the rural population relocates to urban areas.

Dreams are what brought us out here
Dreams of putting our own bread on the table
That's what kept us working
To get to the point where we were barely able
Connie Kaldor from "JUST A LITTLE DREAM"

All that's left of this once vital farmyard are a couple of small, rundown buildings used for storing all manner of old parts and bolts and bits of iron. Can we imagine the hardship and hurt, but also the laughter and joy that was experienced here so many years ago?

How many of these old hand pumps were sold and installed on farms all over the prairies before running water and indoor plumbing became the norm? How fondly I remember delightful summers spent on my grandparents' farm as a young boy – the cool well house and the icy-cold artesian well water that flowed from it.

▲   *There are several places on the prairies where oil well pump jacks like this have been installed over the last few decades as our technological society has become more dependent on fossil fuels. Although there are still large reserves of non-renewable resources left on earth, they are not the limitless sources of energy we once thought they were.*

▶   *Sometimes something as simple as raindrops beading on a patch of oily pavement can make an interesting photograph. If you look closely, you can see the photographer's reflection in each drop.*

A pair of Great Horned Owls have a nest in this old barn and are often seen sitting in this window; one or the other of them, or sometimes both together. Almost as large as the Great Grey Owl, the Great Horned Owl is a formidable hunter, willing and able to attack medium-sized mammals and birds such as porcupine, skunk, duck, and grouse.

A Great Grey Owl, North America's largest owl, peers at me around a tree trunk. He seemed completely unconcerned with my presence until I tried to move in too close, then he spread his wings and left the scene in a silent glide just above the forest floor.

A field of oat sheaf stooks brings back memories of long days and hard work to many who remember what harvest was like during the first third of this century. The binder is not often used these days except for old-time threshing demonstrations, or by the occasional old-timer who does so "just for the hell of it".

Hey Joe, what'cha gonna grow,
It's nearly time to seed,
I don't know, a quarter in oats,
But the rest it goes to wheat

Connie Kaldor from "SPRING IN THE PRAIRIES"

You just hope you can hold on so
You don't end up like the neighbours
Him and her they're weeping as the auctioneer yells
 Connie Kaldor from "HARSH AND UNFORGIVING"

Two old tractors from a much earlier era, saved from the scrap heap, let us peer back briefly into a much harder but also a much slower and quieter time. No comparison to today's monsters, but is that good or bad?

Autumn, harvest, and haying all go hand in hand on the prairies. At New Roots, here in the Touchwood Hills of east central Saskatchewan, late afternoon backlighting adds a warm golden glow.

The smell of hay
When the sun goes down
Is something like a symphony
And the smell of that hay
With the things you say
Are stirring up more than memory
Connie Kaldor from "CALAIS MAINE"

70

You can work all year
You can get it in the bin
There's no telling what price you get or if it sells
    Connie Kaldor from "HARSH AND UNFORGIVING"

Harvesting on the prairies today is not nearly as labor intensive as it used to be. On the other hand, the total energy input required to produce a bushel of grain in our modern world is much greater than the energy derived from that same bushel of grain.

▲   *Poplars and prairie grasses show various stages of color changes as the nights get colder and winter approaches. The many splotches of green, red, yellow, and brown blend as if someone had splattered the landscape with the flick of a very large paintbrush.*

▶   *Fall on the prairies is an extraordinary time of year, with gorgeous autumn colors; clear, crisp air; bright, warm days; and cool nights. The wonderful light we often get in the autumn has always drawn me, as a photographer, to try and transfer these beautiful images to film. A deep blue sky helps to enhance the photo.*

◄   *Every farmer's dream is a bin full of gold at the end of the rainbow. The precious metal would be nice but a bin full of high quality, dry grain after a good harvest will do.*

▶   *Special conditions often make all the difference. A photo of an elevator and an old farmyard is nothing special until it's framed by a beautiful dark sky and an intensely bright rainbow. Notice how the rainbow seems to divide the sky into two distinct parts.*

Early morning light on a bright, clear, late summer day adds texture and depth to flatland grain crops south of Saskatoon as farmers get an early start on the day's swathing. I traded the pilot a photograph of his farm for this chance to see the beautiful harvest patterns from a unique perspective. To get crisp, clear photos we wired the plane window open before leaving the ground.

The beaver is North America's largest rodent and Canada's national emblem. It spends half its life swimming and much of the rest building dams. The deeper water behind these dams ensures access to the lodges through underwater entrances during winter months. Trapped almost to extinction a century ago for its fine, dense fur, the beaver is making a comeback thanks to protection laws and a decline in the demand for furs.

Many people consider beavers to be a nuisance because of the damage they do to forests, but the dams and ponds they build also help control flooding and provide habitat for hundreds of other water-loving creatures.

Deep autumn colors reflected in a large, bright beaver pond produce a sort of abstraction of reality. The beaver swimming across the foreground pulls us back to the real world and reminds us why the pond is there in the first place.

The early autumn leaves of a Red-osier Dogwood add a splash of bright color to a small poplar bluff beside a country road. The dogwood is common throughout central North America and is one of the plants that makes the fall display on the prairies so spectacular.

The Whooping Crane, so close to extinction for so long and still a long way from flourishing, is, nevertheless, slowly increasing in numbers.

A magnificent bird, especially in flight, with a two and a half meter (7 ½ ft.) wingspan, the Whooping Crane is a wary bird and is seen on the prairies only during migration in the spring and fall. I took these photographs at Little Quill Lake during the fall migration.

By far the most common bear in North America, the Black Bear has one of the most extensive ranges of any large animal on the continent. With a coat varying in color from totally black through various shades of brown, the Black Bear can climb trees easily and sprint as fast as fifty-five kilometers per hour (34 mph.). Contrary to popular belief, bears do not hibernate, but rather become lethargic and dormant during the winter months. Metabolism rate and body temperature do not change as sharply as in true hibernation.

Timber Wolves, in my mind some of the most beautiful animals in North America, are intelligent and strong, displaying a grace possessed by few other species. Much maligned and feared in a way they've never deserved, they now exist in numbers only in the North. Even there they are threatened by humans, who feel a need to control everything – including nature.

A single cattail flower remains from the previous year, as new spring growth begins in the water below. Side lighting from a low early-morning sun causes the subject to stand out against the dark, out-of-focus background.

Winter cattails stand to attention after a late spring snowstorm has again turned the bare landscape a brilliant white. The fifteen to twenty centimeters (6 - 8 in.) of heavy, wet snow turned the water to slush in which the returning geese left footprints as they took flight.

A heavy buildup of hoarfrost produces a fairyland effect over this cross-country ski trail. Cold temperatures and very light winds allowed the frost to build up over a period of two days.

A walk on the golf course on a cold winter morning can provide scenes that no golfer is ever likely to see. Here the sun is just up after a night of heavy hoarfrost, creating a simple beauty that many of us on the prairies fail to notice or appreciate.

▲   Sundogs are similar to rainbows in that they are the result of refracted and reflected sunlight. The difference is that rainbows are produced by water droplets in the air in the summer, while sundogs are produced by ice crystals in the air, usually in very cold weather. Sundogs are beautiful, but can be hard to look at, and are sometimes difficult to photograph due to the brightness of the sun.

I'm not the kind to sit and pine
For places far away
. . . But something about the moon tonight
Sent a longing to my soul
Connie Kaldor from
"MARGARET'S WALTZ"

▶   Early winter, and a light, even snowfall over this stubble field looks blue with the reflection from the cold, dark early-morning sky. To get a properly exposed moon into the photo, I had to superimpose a separate image during the printing process.

Many parts of the prairies owe much of their heritage to people of the Ukraine who settled here during the early part of this century, looking for a better life. The unique domed churches they built add beauty and interest to the landscape, even in a late spring snowstorm.

I was a young girl
When I came to this land
From a country far away
To a language I didn't understand

I worked on a farm
And I married a man
We got ourselves a homestead
On a section of land

Connie Kaldor from "GRANDMOTHER'S SONG"

When I arrived home at 5:30 a.m. New Year's morning, from a quiet, private party, the trees, fences, and grass were all loaded with up to four centimeters (1 ½ in.) of fluffy, white hoarfrost. I was up again with the sun and took photos until noon, when the frost began to drop off.

On my way to look for crocuses to photograph in the snow during a late spring storm in May, I was stopped at a railway crossing by an approaching train. I quickly grabbed my camera and took this shot out of the truck window.

Winter stays so long
Seems like it always has been
Connie Kaldor from "SPRING IN THE PRAIRIES"

A spring snowstorm on the prairies can sometimes be as fierce and heavy as any during the winter. This one, in late March, was not a raging blizzard, but fifteen to twenty centimeters (6 - 8 in.) of heavy, wet snow had accumulated before it was over. Photographers sometimes need to do crazy things to get the right shot. For this one, I had to set up the tripod on top of the truck cab to get the right angle.

A cold, windswept small-town cemetery is not the most pleasant place in the middle of winter; however, there is a certain hypnotic draw to the regularity of the frosty tombstones and shadowed drifts.

This is not a world for the gentle of heart
I see so many buck the trend
And they fall apart
And they go too soon
The gentle of heart

Connie Kaldor from "GENTLE OF HEART"

High humidity during a cold winter night has condensed, crystal by crystal, onto a thin blade of grass to build up nearly three centimeters (1 in.) of dense, white hoarfrost. The frost has also collected on the snow, making the snowbanks look like piles of popcorn.

An animal path in the snow seems to lead us deep into the forested parkland near Kelvington, Saskatchewan. This photo was taken on a cold and frosty, but beautifully calm day, while we were on our annual Christmas tree hunt.

Whenever I travel through forest during the winter months, I am constantly looking for scenes of quiet beauty. Not too many come together as well as this one.

Aurora borealis, popularly known as the northern lights, are often visible over much of the prairies, especially on very cold winter nights – at least that's the way it seems when I'm trying to get good photos. Sometimes they are barely visible and hardly seem to move at all. At other times they are extremely bright and colorful, and literally dance all over the sky. It's at times like these that they are the most awe inspiring, but also the hardest to photograph. Because they change so quickly, they don't record properly on the slower speed films.

Stop. I had help with this photograph, taken in the badlands of South Dakota. I was about to get into the car and drive away, when my travelling companion said, "Look at the stop sign!". The photo was taken under existing light conditions, looking east, just seconds before the sun dropped below the horizon in the west.

Because film cannot register nearly as wide a range of light and dark as the human eye can perceive, we must constantly be aware of what we want the main interest in a photo to be. Exposing for glaring wet pavement after a summer shower, darkens everything in the background and makes it appear as if this photo was taken in the middle of the night.